Why do I Need to Read?

Jane Medwell

Contents

Invitations 3
Books 4
Newspapers 6
TV guides 7
Signs 8
Buses 9
Telephone directories 10
Fun! 11
Index 12

OXFORD
UNIVERSITY PRESS

OXFORD
UNIVERSITY PRESS

Great Clarendon Street, Oxford, OX2 6DP

Oxford University Press is a department of the University of Oxford.
It furthers the University's objective of excellence in research, scholarship,
and education by publishing worldwide in

Oxford New York

Athens Auckland Bangkok Bogotá Buenos Aires Calcutta
Cape Town Chennai Dar es Salaam Delhi Florence Hong Kong Istanbul
Karachi Kuala Lumpur Madrid Melbourne Mexico City Mumbai
Nairobi Paris São Paulo Singapore Taipei Tokyo Toronto Warsaw

with associated companies in Berlin Ibadan

Oxford is a registered trade mark of Oxford University Press
in the UK and in certain other countries

Text © Jane Medwell 1999

The moral rights of the author have been asserted

Database right Oxford University Press (maker)

First published by Oxford University Press 1999
Reprinted 1999

All rights reserved. No part of this publication may be reproduced,
stored in a retrieval system, or transmitted, in any form or by any means,
without the prior permission in writing of Oxford University Press, or as
expressly permitted by law, or under terms agreed with the appropriate
reprographics rights organization. Enquiries concerning reproduction
outside the scope of the above should be sent to the Rights Department,
Oxford University Press, at the address above

You must not circulate this book in any other binding or cover
and you must impose this same condition on any acquirer

A CIP record for this book is available from the British Library

ISBN 0 19 915753 7
Available in packs
Pack A Pack of Six   (one of each book)   ISBN 0 19 915756 1
Pack A Class Pack   (six of each book)   ISBN 0 19 915757 X

Printed in Hong Kong

Acknowledgements

The publisher would like to thank the following for permission
to reproduce photographs: Corel Professional Photos: p 9 (bottom);
Corbis UK Ltd/Philip James Corwin: p 9 (top); Corbis UK Ltd/Dave G Houser:
p 8 (top); Corbis UK Ltd/Joseoh Sohm: p 8 (bottom); Martin Sookias: p 11.

All other photography by Mark Mason

With thanks to St Barnabas School, Oxford

Front cover photograph by Martin Sookias
Back cover photograph by Mark Mason

Invitations

You need to read to find out where the party is.

Books

You need to read to find information.

What is ....

the environment?
Our environment is our surroundings. Some environments are natural, others have been made by people. People have damaged the natural environment in many parts of the world.

a mountain?
A mountain is a very high hill. Mountains often have steep slopes, and can be rocky or covered with snow.

a desert?
A desert is dry land with few plants. Deserts are often sandy, or covered with stones or bare rock.

a forest?
A forest is a very large area of trees. Cold forests have fir or pine trees. Hot forests have thick jungle.

savannah?
Savannah lands have tall grass and few trees. They are very warm and have a rainy season and a dry season.

a marsh?
A marsh is low, wet land. Marshes are often found next to lakes, rivers or the sea.

ice?
Ice is frozen water. Very large areas of ice on the land are called ice caps. Very large lumps of ice in the sea are called icebergs.

Cleaning your hamster's cage

Every day

1 Clean out your hamster's droppings.

2 Wash its feeding bowl and water bottle, and give it fresh water.

Once a week

1 Clean the whole cage out and throw away the floor covering and bedding.

You need to read instructions to find out how to do things.

Newspapers

You need to read to find out what's happening.

TV guides

You need to read to find out what time your programme is on.

Signs

You need to read to find out where to go.

Buses

You need to read to find out where the bus is going.

Telephone directories

You need to read to find out your friend's telephone number.

Fun!

You can read just to have fun!

Index

a

b books 4
buses 9

c

d

e

f friend 10
fun 11

g

h happening 6

i information 4
instructions 5
invitations 3

j

k

l

m

n newspapers 6

o

p party 3
programme 7

q

r

s signs 8

t telephone
directories 10
tv guides 7

u

v

w where 8, 9

x

y

z